The Facts About Cerebral Palsy

Rachel B. Heimovics

Contents

Rigby®

A Harcourt Achieve Imprint

www.Rigby.com

1-800-531-5015

Muscles at Work

How are a hug and a jump alike? What about playing a game of basketball and climbing stairs? You do them all with the help of your muscles.

Snap your fingers. Did you use your muscles?

You use muscles to snap, clap, shiver, hiccup, laugh, and smile. Muscles make it all happen.

But what would happen if your muscles didn't work the way they should? Could you still do all of these things?

Hugs are just one of the things you can do with your muscles.

There are lots of muscles inside the human body. You have them from the top of your head to the tips of your toes, not just in your arms and legs. There are muscles in your face, your eyes, and even your tongue. And, muscles are some of the largest **organs** you have.

Muscles move your body. Leg muscles make you run and skip, and you use your arm muscles to lift and push things. Neck muscles hold up your head.

Finger muscles help this boy write with his pencil.

Some muscles work because you want them to. Your brain tells your foot to tap, and it does.

But other muscles work on their own without you telling them to. You don't even have to think about them. Some of these muscles are used for breathing and digesting food.

The heart is another example of this kind of muscle. It pumps blood throughout the body. The heart muscle works even when you are asleep.

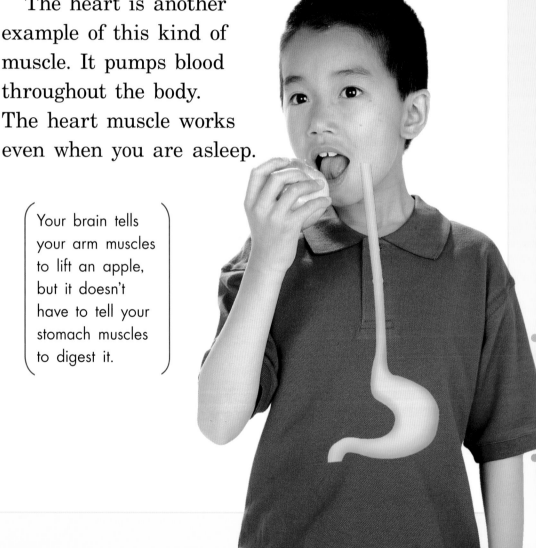

Your brain tells your arm muscles to lift an apple, but it doesn't have to tell your stomach muscles to digest it.

Most muscles are joined to bones. Bones make up your **skeleton**. Your muscles move your skeleton as you walk, run, lift objects, and play. The muscles pull the bones the way you want them to go. If you want to close your hand, your muscles pull the bones of your hand into a fist.

Muscles work as a team. It takes a lot of them to even hold a fork or turn a page in this book. In fact, it takes 17 different muscles just to smile!

This picture shows how the muscles in the girl's arm are attached to the bones. The muscles allow her to pick up the phone.

Commands from the Brain

The brain is the control room for the body. It does all of your thinking and feeling, and it also tells the body to move.

How does the brain control the movements of the body? It sends out **commands** to the muscles. **Nerves** carry these commands from the brain down to all the muscles. These nerves stretch to every part of the body.

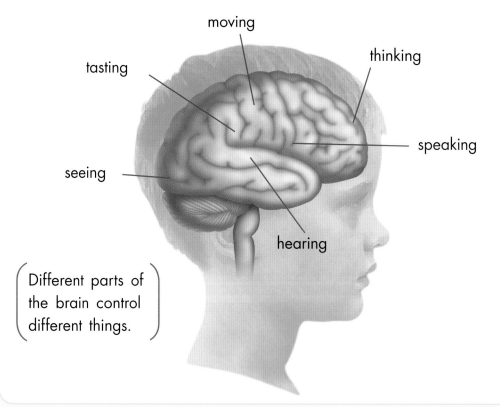

moving

thinking

tasting

speaking

seeing

hearing

Different parts of the brain control different things.

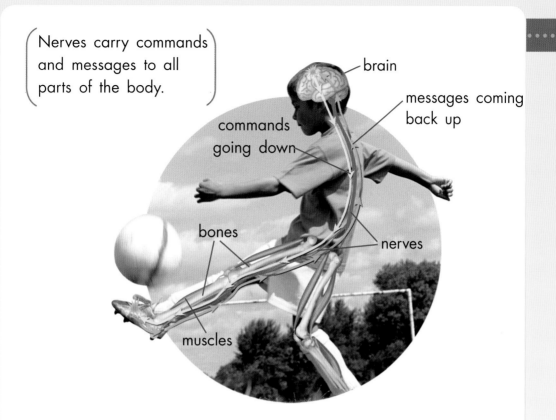

Nerves carry commands and messages to all parts of the body.

brain

messages coming back up

commands going down

bones

nerves

muscles

What happens when you decide to kick a ball? Your brain sends a super fast command through your nerves to the muscles in your leg. This command tells the muscles in your leg to kick the ball.

Messages go both ways. If you kick too hard, you might hurt your foot. If that happens the muscles will send a message back through your nerves up to your brain. You will feel pain.

Fewer Commands

Sometimes the brain can become badly hurt. A person might fall and hit his or her head. Or, the person might be in a bad accident. These kinds of accidents can sometimes cause an **injury** to a person's brain.

Injury to a baby's brain can happen around the time of birth. If the injury is really bad, the brain may not work like it should. It may not be able to send the right commands down to the body. If that happens, then the nerves will not carry the right messages to the muscles.

Brain injuries like this can sometimes cause cerebral palsy, or CP for short.

An injury to any of these three areas of the brain can cause cerebral palsy.

So what is cerebral palsy? *Cerebral* means "having to do with the brain." *Palsy* means "muscles that do not work right."

When a person has cerebral palsy, their muscles get fewer commands from the brain, and also, these commands often do not work right. The muscles do not understand what the brain wants them to do. Sometimes the muscles do nothing. Other times the muscles move, but they do not do what they're supposed to.

This girl gets around with the help of a walker.

Cerebral palsy is not a **disease**. It is caused by an injury to the brain. This kind of injury is different from hurting your leg or breaking your arm. Those kinds of injuries can heal. After a while, your arm bones heal, and you can use your arm again. But injuries to the brain cannot heal. Once the brain is injured, it will not get better.

Arm and leg bones can heal as good as new. But the brain is an organ that cannot heal.

Cerebral palsy most often happens to babies and very young children. A baby's **skull** is not finished growing. It can still be soft in places. Until the skull becomes hard like the rest of the bones, the brain inside the skull can be hurt.

But even if a baby or child has cerebral palsy, he or she can still live a full life. People with CP read, play with their friends, and do everything other people do. They just might do these activities a little differently.

Children with CP enjoy all the fun activities their friends do.

People with CP are not all alike. CP affects people in many different ways.

Some people with CP might have to be in a **wheelchair**, unable to move or speak. Others might only have trouble walking or holding things. And some people have such **mild** CP that you might not even be able to tell that they have it.

Some people with CP have to be in a wheelchair.

Mild CP

Sometimes CP can be very mild. People with mild CP might walk with a limp. They might have trouble grabbing objects, or they might sound a little bit different when they speak.

But this doesn't slow them down. People with mild CP can do just about everything anyone else can do.

This girl's CP is very mild. She wears braces on her legs to help her walk.

Moderate CP

People with **moderate** CP might have trouble walking or standing. They also might have trouble seeing or hearing. If the CP affects the tongue muscle, the person might have a hard time speaking. But even though some people with CP cannot speak, their minds still work fine. They can learn everything other people can.

People with CP who have trouble talking often use special talking computers. These computers "say" things for them.

Many people with moderate CP must have help to walk. This girl uses crutches to get around.

This boy with CP cannot speak. He types what he wants his computer to say for him.

Severe CP

Some people have **severe** CP. They cannot walk or stand at all. They cannot hold up their heads without help. Their legs or arms may jerk around without the person wanting them to.

People with severe CP must use wheelchairs throughout their lives. These wheelchairs have motors in them that the person can control. A control stick is used to drive the chair where the person wants to go.

The headrest on this wheelchair helps support the boy's head.

- Most people with CP had a brain injury around the time of birth.
- Cerebral palsy does not get worse with age, but it never goes away.
- Not all people with CP are alike. Many can do the same things that other people can do.
- Cerebral palsy is not a sickness or a disease. You cannot catch it from someone else.

Many children with CP go to school every day like other children.

Children with CP enjoy many of the same activities as children without CP. Playing with friends, going to the park, and playing games are fun for everyone.

Many children with CP are able to go to the same schools as other children. They are able to learn all of the same things and someday go to college. As adults, they can have great jobs and full lives.

People who have CP will have it their whole lives. Yet there are many things they can do to keep themselves healthy.

A person called a **physical therapist** can help the person with exercises. These exercises keep muscles strong and fit.

Those who have trouble speaking often go to a **speech-language therapist**. This is a person that helps people learn to speak the best that they can.

Therapists help people with CP and other disabilities stay happy and healthy.

Physical Therapist

Speech-language Therapist

The story of how Bill Porter (right) became a salesman was made into a movie on TV. Here he meets William H. Macy, the actor who played him in the movie.

People with CP learn to live with their **disability**. They don't let it keep them from doing the things they want. For example, a man named Bill Porter was born with CP. As an adult, he was told over and over again that no one would give him a job.

Well, Bill proved everybody wrong. He became a salesman. Over time, he worked hard and became the top salesman at his company. Bill's story was even turned into a movie!

Some people with CP even become actors and actresses. Geri Jewell was an actress on a television show called *The Facts of Life*. She was the first person with a disability to have a leading part on a TV show.

Today, Geri is a comedian and public speaker who speaks to people all over the country. She shows everyone that even though you have a disability, you can still have a successful and happy life.

Despite her disability, Geri Jewell is a successful comedian and public speaker.

Wrap Up

Cerebral palsy is an injury to the brain. It most often happens to babies and very young children. This injury makes it hard for the brain to tell the muscles what to do.

But people with CP can have very happy lives. They go to school, get jobs, and even become stars. In fact, with a little help and a whole lot of hard work, they can still follow their dreams.

This girl may grow up to work with animals one day!

command an order to do something

disability not able to do something

disease a bad illness

injury a hurt, cut, or break to a part of the body

mild not bad

moderate in the middle

nerve the part of the body that carries commands from the brain

organ a part of the body such as the heart or kidney

physical therapist a person who helps
people exercise

severe very bad

skeleton all the bones of the body

skull the bone in a person's head

speech-language therapist a person who
helps people speak better

wheelchair a special chair with wheels
that's used by people who can't walk